THE ELIZABETHANS

R. D. LOBBAN

Illustrated by Clyde Pearson

University of London Press Ltd

942·055:3   31·1·69

University of London Press Ltd
St Paul's House, Warwick Lane, London EC4

Map on page 13 by Crispin Fisher
Printed and bound in England by
Hazell Watson & Viney Ltd, Aylesbury, Bucks

THE ELIZABETHANS

Contents

1 · *The Elizabethan Adventurers*

THE English seamen moved forward stealthily in the darkness towards the port of Nombre de Dios. Then when they were only about a mile from the town, their leader, Francis Drake, brought them to a halt. Without a sound the men took up positions in hiding at the side of the trail.

Slowly the minutes dragged past. At last the sky away to the east began to lighten. Anxiously Drake and his men peered along the trail, but still there was no sign of the Spanish mule train.

The year was 1573, and Drake and his men were hoping to seize Spanish treasure. The Spaniards mined huge quantities of gold in South America and shipped it up the west coast to Panama. The gold was then taken overland across the Isthmus of Panama on mule trains to Nombre de Dios. From there it was shipped in great convoys across the Atlantic to Spain.

Drake, the son of a Devonshire farmer and one of the greatest English seamen of the day, had discovered that the mule trains were only lightly guarded. He had planned an expedition to seize one of them, and only a short time before he and his men had landed from their ship. Native guides had led them to this spot near Nombre de Dios to prepare an ambush.

Suddenly through the still morning air came the sounds of jangling and chiming bells. The mule train was approaching along the trail! Soon the leading animals were abreast of the seamen's position. Yet none of the Englishmen stirred, and the unsuspecting Spaniards moved along past the place where they were hidden.

And then at a signal from Drake the seamen sprang into action. A few of them seized the leading mules, while the others attacked

the Spanish guards. There were about fifty Spanish soldiers and they fought bravely. But after a brief struggle they fled towards Nombre de Dios. Drake and his men were left with all the booty.

The haul was beyond their wildest dreams. There were almost 200 mules laden with gold, silver and precious jewels. They could not carry all the treasure away with them, and so they buried the silver. The gold and the jewels they loaded on to their shoulders and then they hurried off into the woods. Spaniards from Nombre de Dios gave chase, but they were unable to catch up with them. Soon Drake and his men were safely aboard their ship and on their way home to England.

At the time of this raid on the Spanish mule train, England and Spain were still at peace in Europe, but in the lands across the Atlantic they were fierce rivals and enemies. In 1492 Columbus had discovered the West Indies, and this led to Spain building up a great empire in the "new" continent of America. She claimed almost all of the lands as her own, and declared that no foreigners could settle there or even trade with the Spanish colonies.

THE AGE OF ELIZABETH   At first Englishmen had been too busy with troubles at home to take much interest in the New World, although John Cabot had reached it in 1497. But during the reign of Queen Elizabeth (1558–1603) English seamen, traders and explorers became much more active. A new Age had begun, when English ships and sailors would sail on every ocean and England would become one of the greatest nations of the world. We now call this period the Age of Elizabeth, since the Queen herself did so much to make all the triumphs and successes possible. Her subjects are known as the Elizabethans.

The Elizabethans were certainly not prepared to be shut out of the trade with the New World. They defied the Spaniards and sent out ships to obtain gold, jewels and sugar from the Spanish colonies. One of the first men to embark on this trade was John Hawkins, the son of a Plymouth merchant. In 1562 he sailed to Africa, and from there he carried large numbers of negro slaves across the Atlantic. The Spanish settlers were only too willing to buy the slaves, for they needed them to work on their sugar plantations, but the Spanish government would permit only their own merchants to carry goods and slaves to their colonies. Galleons were sent out to seize the English ships, and any seamen who fell into the hands of the Spaniards were executed as pirates.

Naturally the actions of the Spaniards angered the English. Instead of trying to trade with the Spanish colonies, they began to attack and plunder Spanish possessions and Spanish treasure ships. Drake's successful attack on the mule train encouraged other English seamen to follow his example.

VOYAGE ROUND THE WORLD   Drake himself soon began to make plans for another expedition. This time he proposed sailing to the Pacific Ocean where there were fabulous riches to be won. No English captain had ever ventured into the Pacific before, and the Spaniards believed they were completely safe from attack there. Their treasure ships therefore sailed unescorted and practically unarmed up the west coast of America to Panama.

In 1577 Drake set out with five ships. He headed south-west towards the Strait of Magellan, but as he passed through this feared stretch of water, the ships were scattered in a fierce storm. Drake in the *Pelican* (later named the *Golden Hind*) eventually struggled through to the Pacific, but the other ships were certain that he had been lost, and they turned back.

Undismayed, Drake sailed north and plundered the ports of Valparaiso and Lima. At Lima he learnt that a great treasure ship named *Our Lady of the Conception* had only recently sailed. He immediately set off in pursuit, and after an exciting chase the Spanish ship was overtaken and boarded. Immense treasure was taken, and for two days the English seamen gleefully poured a stream of gold, silver and jewels into the holds of the *Golden Hind*. To this day no one knows the value of the plunder, but it would certainly be worth much more than £2,000,000 of our present-day money.

Drake in the Strait of Magellan

Now that the Spaniards were aware of his presence, Drake decided to return to England. He headed across the Pacific, and made his way home by the Spice Islands, the Indian Ocean and the Cape of Good Hope. He reached Plymouth in 1580, and thus became the first Englishman to have sailed round the world. Queen Elizabeth was so delighted with his exploits that she visited the ship and knighted Drake on the quarter-deck.

NORTH-WEST AND NORTH-EAST PASSAGES   Not all Englishmen wished to take part in raids against the Spaniards, and many would have preferred to continue peaceful trading. They tried to send out ships to the lands of the Far East with their rich silks and spices, but here, too, they found obstacles in the way. The Spaniards controlled the route round south America or the one across the Isthmus of Panama, and would not allow the ships of other nations to pass. The route round Africa to India was blocked by the Portuguese who had set up several bases along the African coast.

The English merchants were forced to search for another sea

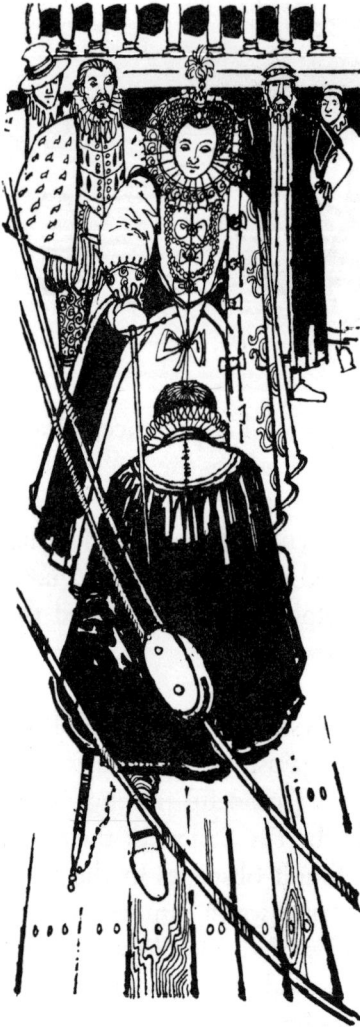

Queen Elizabeth knighting Drake

route to India and the East. Not having very much knowledge of the geography of the world, they believed that it might be possible to sail round the north of Canada or round the north of Russia. These proposed routes were known as the North-West and the North-East Passages, and from the early 1550's onwards several attempts were made to discover them. But always the terrible Arctic winters to the north of Canada and Russia defeated the English explorers and they could find no way through the ice-bound Arctic seas.

FROBISHER   One of the most famous of the Elizabethan explorers was Martin Frobisher. He led the first English expedition to search for the North-West Passage in 1576, and in all he made three voyages. He thought he had found a way through to the Pacific, but the opening he discovered was only a great bay, now known as Frobisher Bay.

12

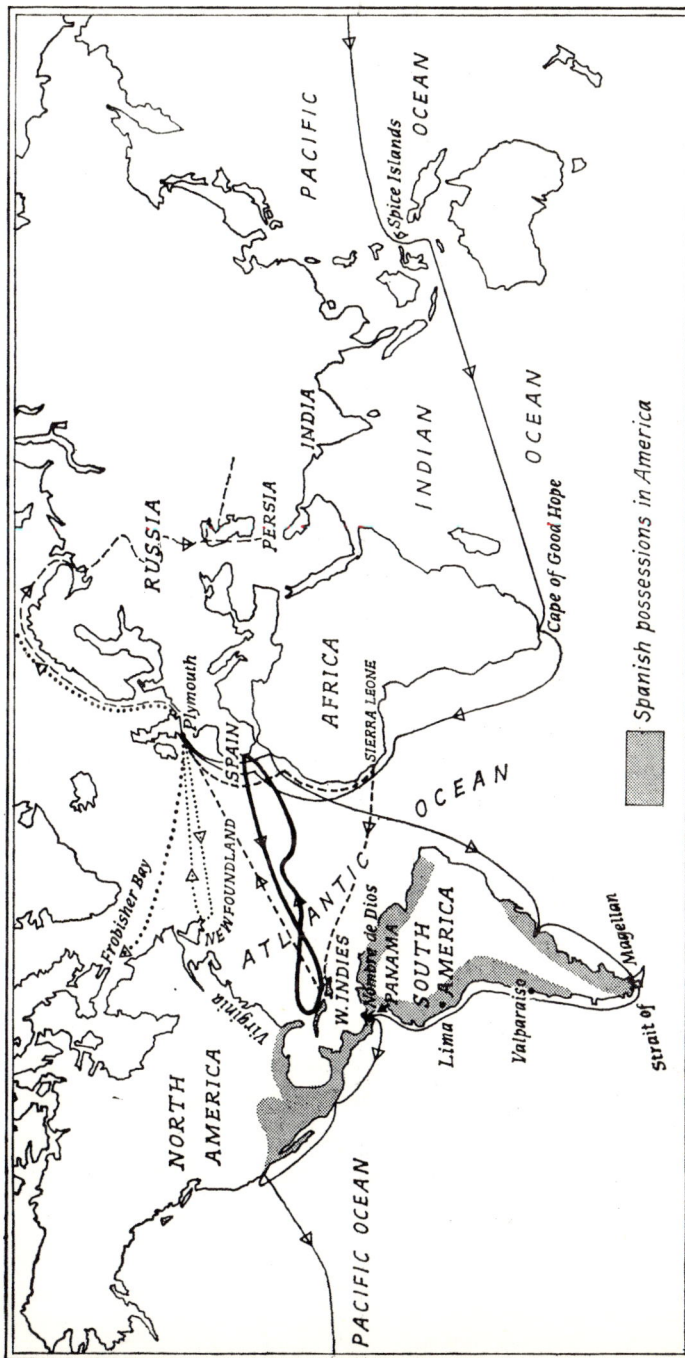

Cabot's route [1497]	Hawkins's route [1562] ---
Drake's route [1577-80]——	Jenkinson's route [1557-58] ─ · ─ · ─
Columbus's route [1492] ——	N.E. Passage route and
	N.W. Passage route ············

Spanish possessions in America

OVERLAND ROUTE   While the sailors were attempting to discover a North-West or a North-East Passage, other Englishmen were trying with more success to open up a route to the East by land. In 1557 and 1561 the great explorer Anthony Jenkinson made two amazing journeys across Russia and Western Asia to Persia. There the Shah threatened to have him executed because he was a Christian, but Jenkinson talked himself out of his dangerous situation and even persuaded the Shah to make a trade agreement with him.

TRADING COMPANIES   To develop trade with the islands which Jenkinson and other explorers had opened up, a company known as the Muscovy Company was founded by some English merchants. Soon other trading companies were formed, among them the Eastland Company to trade with countries bordering the Baltic Sea, and the Levant Company to trade with the Mediterranean lands. Most famous of all was the East India Company founded in 1600 which was later to play an important part in building up the British Empire in India.

COLONIES   As their trade with other lands developed, the Elizabethans became more and more interested in setting up colonies overseas. In 1583 Sir Humphrey Gilbert sailed with colonists to Newfoundland, while in 1585 and 1587 Sir Walter Raleigh made two attempts to establish a colony which he named Virginia. Unfortunately all three expeditions ended in failure, and no further attempts were made to found colonies in Elizabeth's reign. They did have some good results, however, for it was probably Raleigh's settlers who first brought back potatoes and the tobacco plant to England.

ELIZABETHAN SHIPS   Despite their failure to set up colonies, the Elizabethans were certainly magnificent sailors and adventurers. Their voyages and exploits are all the more admirable to us when we realise just how small and frail their ships actually were. Drake's ship, the *Golden Hind*, was smaller than a modern fishing boat, being only about 100 tons, yet in this craft he sailed round the world and defied all the fleets of Spain.

Conditions aboard the Elizabethan sailing ships were often extremely unpleasant. The captain and a few of the officers might sleep in cabins, but the ordinary sailors were crammed all together in the fo'c'sle or below deck. They slept on the bare deck wrapped in rough blankets or coats. In winter on the seas of Europe they would freeze with cold, while in the tropics they would endure agonies from the fierce heat.

FOOD   The diet of the Elizabethan seamen could be quite appalling. At the beginning of a voyage they had supplies of bacon, biscuits, dried fish, beer and cider, but as the weeks passed the meat began to smell and became foul-tasting, and the beer tasted more and more like vinegar.

On a long voyage the daily rations usually became steadily smaller. The captain might have calculated that he had enough supplies to feed his crew, but if the ship happened to be blown off course or was delayed by contrary winds, then the crew suffered real hunger. On one occasion Hawkins' crew were so hungry that they ate all their pets and were even forced to go hunting in the holds for rats!

DISCIPLINE   Life on board an Elizabethan ship involved a great deal of hard work, for a sailing ship was much more difficult to handle than a modern steam or diesel-driven vessel. Discipline was very strict, and even for a minor offence a seaman would receive a severe flogging. Those who mutinied or refused to obey orders were instantly hanged. Many captains also introduced a large number of rules and regulations which the men had to obey. On Hawkins' ship each man had to attend daily prayers, and anyone who was absent was put in irons.

DISEASE   Life at sea could also be very dangerous for the Elizabethan seamen, even if they were fortunate enough to keep clear of a superior force of Spanish galleons. It was always a hazardous task to climb the rigging during a storm, and accidents were frequent. There were also many diseases that attacked men on board ship. One of the commonest was scurvy, a painful skin disease brought on by the lack of vegetables and fresh fruit. In the tropics there were several deadly fevers that could strike down almost all the men on a ship. On one of Drake's voyages two of his brothers and more than half of the ship's company perished.

Yet in spite of all the dangers, many Elizabethans were ready and willing to set sail from England in search of adventure and wealth. Some were lucky and did return home with a fortune, but others came ashore penniless and disabled. But even for a crippled beggar it must have been a fine thing to be able to tell all his neighbours that he had been with Drake at Nombre de Dios or with Frobisher among the ice-floes.

2 · *Elizabethan England*

ONDON   The England that sent adventurers to strange, romantic, far-off places during the reign of Elizabeth was itself a land full of colour and interest. London, the capital, was a fascinating city, and many visitors from abroad came to see its splendours. It was much smaller than it is now, its boundaries being the old city wall with gates at Aldgate, Ludgate, Moorgate, Cripplegate, Aldersgate and Bishopsgate, and to the south the River Thames. But already London was bursting out beyond its bounds, and many houses were being built outside the walls. Each year hundreds flocked to it in the hope of winning fame and fortune, and by 1600 it had grown to be a prosperous city of some 200,000 people.

With its fast-growing population, Elizabethan London seemed to be permanently crowded. There were some lovely gardens and orchards along the river, but most of the city consisted of narrow, cobbled streets thronged with people. During the day many workmen were to be seen erecting new buildings or repairing old ones. Women bargained with the shopkeepers or merely gossiped with their friends. Merchants hurried past to their place of business at the Royal Exchange, while porters carrying heavy burdens elbowed passers-by aside. A continuous stream of carts and coaches rattled its way dangerously through the streets.

Vendors were everywhere crying their wares. Here an old lady calls: "Cherry ripe, apples fine"; there a flower seller presses a buttonhole on a young dandy dressed in his finery. Further along a young girl smiles happily as she sells oranges from Seville. Suddenly an urchin darts forward towards her basket, but she is quicker than he is. He retreats in dismay, rubbing his smarting ear.

Elizabethan London had many fine buildings, the most notable perhaps being St. Peter's Abbey, the Royal Exchange, St. Paul's Church and the Queen's Palace at Whitehall. St. Paul's was a famous landmark, and visitors gathered there in large numbers to see the booksellers and merchants carrying on their business in the Churchyard. Then they paid their penny and climbed up to the top of the steeple to view the river and the surrounding countryside. Unfortunately the steeple was burnt down in 1561, and the

Abbey was also destroyed in the Great Fire of London in 1666.

Perhaps the most popular attraction for visitors to the city was the great Bridge across the Thames. It had twenty arches and was jammed tight with a double row of shops and houses. A rather gruesome feature was the gatehouse tower, for this was the place where the government chose to display the heads of traitors. Duke Frederick of Wurtemberg when visiting the city in 1593 counted thirty-four heads hanging there on poles as he passed by!

There were other aspects of Elizabethan London that we today would dislike. People dumped their garbage outside their houses, and when it rained the streets became a mass of foul-smelling mud. It was almost impossible to walk through the streets in fine clothes and keep them clean, and many people preferred to travel by water. This was quite easy, for there were several landing stages on the Thames and large numbers of boats plying for hire.

HOUSING   Many of the houses in Elizabethan London were almost as insanitary as the streets. The typical dwellings of the

ordinary people had three, four and five storeys. Underneath was a cellar, and on the top storey was a garret. Often the upper storeys jutted out over the lower ones making the streets and alleyways dark and gloomy.

Originally one family might have occupied such a building, living in the upper storeys and using the ground floor as their shop and workrooms. But as more and more people flocked into London, the houses became increasingly overcrowded and several families would live all huddled together on each floor. Soon the buildings became littered with filth and dirt, and children played among the heaps of garbage in the alleyways. Rats were to be found everywhere, and the fleas which bred on them spread disease and plague through the city.

EMPLOYMENT   Though housing conditions were far from good, London was certainly a thriving, prosperous city, offering employment in a wide variety of trades and occupations. There were merchants, shopkeepers, weavers, tailors, shoemakers, haberdashers, goldsmiths, jewellers and many other workers. The men in each trade tended to live and work all together in one part of the city. The bakers were to be found in Bread Street, the fishmongers on Fish Street Hill, the goldsmiths in Goldsmith Row, and the haberdashers on London Bridge.

All the men in a particular trade, whether they were employers or workmen, were members of an association called a gild. If a youth wished to learn a trade, then he was apprenticed to a craftsman for seven years. At the end of his apprenticeship he had to submit a specimen of his work to the gild to prove that he was a competent tradesman. Apprentices had a reputation for wildness, and they were frequently involved in riots in the city.

THE THEATRE   London was both a place where people could obtain work and also a city with plenty of entertainment. There were many famous inns which on most evenings were thronged with people singing, drinking and dancing. South of the river, at Bankside, stood several theatres. Some of the best-known were the Swan, the Rose and the Globe.

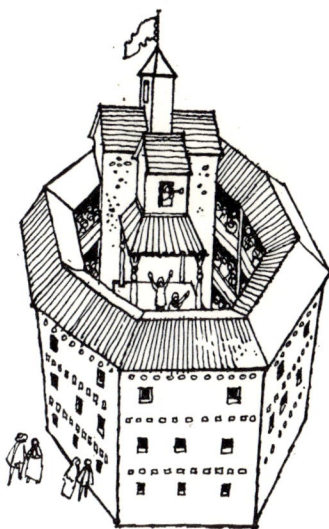

The Globe Theatre

A typical Elizabethan theatre was circular or rectangular in shape and built of wood. Most of the building was uncovered, and the ordinary theatre-goers paid 1d. to stand in the open air. Round the sides were three tiers of enclosed galleries where the wealthier patrons could sit in shelter, and some young gentlemen would pay extra to sit on the side of the stage. There was a balcony above the stage, but there were no curtains. Since there was no stage lighting, the plays were always performed during the hours of daylight.

Some of the plays given at the Elizabethan theatres were written by such famous playwrights as Ben Jonson and Shakespeare. The audiences found Shakespeare's plays exciting and amusing, and during the performances they loved to shout and make humorous remarks. When a favourite actor was recognised, he would be greeted with welcoming cheers. The actors often played pranks on each other, and frequently they engaged in rough horse-play.

BEAR–BAITING AND COCK–FIGHTING Other popular places of entertainment in Elizabethan London were the bear-baiting and cock-fighting pits at Bankside. On Sundays and holidays these pits were always crowded, for the Elizabethans seem to have loved cruel sports. They would shout themselves hoarse as two cockerels with iron claws fixed to their legs tore savagely at each other or as a pack of snarling and snapping dogs attacked an angry bear tethered to a stake. If the bear was quick and alert, it would hurl the dogs violently aside, but if it were too slow, then the dogs would rip viciously into its flesh. Queen Elizabeth was very fond of watching bear-baiting, and often took foreign guests along to the pits.

OTHER TOWNS   Apart from London, there were several other towns in England that were becoming important and prosperous. They were all very much smaller than the capital, but there were a few like York, Bristol and Norwich that had somewhere between 10,000 and 20,000 inhabitants. Bristol had developed a flourishing overseas trade and Norwich had become an important centre of the clothing industry.

INDUSTRIES   The woollen industry at this time was expanding rapidly in East Anglia, Somerset, Yorkshire and Lancashire. Most of the work was still carried out by people spinning and weaving in their own homes. Other industries such as thread-making, lace manufacture, silk-weaving, engraving, the iron industry, and coal mining were all being developed. The coal industry flourished particularly in Northumberland and Durham, while the iron industry was centred in Birmingham and Sussex.

ROADS   With all the developments in trade and industry, it is rather surprising to find that there had been no real improvement made to the roads and means of transport. In winter roads were mere mud tracks, while in summer travellers were often completely covered in dust. Coaches and carts were little better than in medieval times: they had no springs, and still ran on rickety wooden wheels.

Many areas of the country through which the roads ran were as little changed as the tracks themselves. The villages with their clusters of wattle and daub huts and the three great open fields stretching out on all sides were almost exactly the same as they had been for the past 300 years. In some parts of the country, too, there were still great stretches of wasteland or forest with few paths crossing them. Lancashire was three parts marshland, Cannock Chase in Staffordshire was still a great oak forest, while between Brandon and Peterborough there was an enormous stretch of fenland covering more than 3,000 acres.

ENCLOSURES   Yet it would be wrong to think that only in the towns was progress being made. In parts of Kent, Essex, Norfolk, Warwickshire, Worcestershire and elsewhere the great open fields of feudal times were fast disappearing. The development of the clothing industry caused a rise in the price of wool, and farmers and landowners found it very profitable to rear sheep. The open fields were quite unsuited to this type of farming, and therefore landlords began to enclose their land. They formed the strips into large consolidated farms and holdings which were enclosed with hedges or dykes. The villagers now had all their land together instead of in scattered strips.

COUNTRY HOUSES   With the profits they made from sheep-rearing, some of the larger farmers decided to build fine new houses for themselves. Moreton Hall in Cheshire is a good example of the type of building they erected. The framework was made of upright black timbers and cross spars, and the spaces between were filled with lath and white plaster. Unlike the draughty and smoky manors of the Middle Ages, these houses had attractive lattice windows and well-constructed chimneys.

MANSIONS   Even more impressive were the mansions built by wealthy nobles. These were two- or three-storey buildings, often

with fanciful turrets and battlements. They had great oriel windows, and all the stonework was decorated with tracery and carving. Normally they were surrounded by terraces and beautifully laid-out gardens such as at Wayford Manor, Somerset.

INTERIORS   The interiors of these houses were equally grand. On the

ground floor were the kitchens, a dining-room for the owner
and his family, and an enormous hall capable of seating hundreds
of guests. A magnificently carved staircase led up to the second
floor. Here were situated the bedrooms, the great chamber for
entertaining important guests, and a long gallery that was
sometimes over 200 feet in length.

All the living rooms were richly decorated. The ceilings were
plastered and embossed with patterns and designs. Tapestries
covered the walls of the great chamber and the hall, and family
portraits hung in the gallery. The bedrooms, though plainer in
style, had posies or sayings on the walls. Some of these were meant
to give good advice, but the guests might not really have been
very pleased to find a verse like this staring at them from their
bedroom wall:

"With curtain some make scabbard clean, with coverlet their
  shoes;
All dirt and mire some wallow bed, as spaniels use to do."

FURNITURE   The various rooms were also tastefully furnished.
The chairs, stools, chests, cabinets and tables were intricately carved
by highly skilled craftsmen. The most expensive pieces of furniture
were elaborate four-poster beds which cost over £1,000 in our
present-day money. Feather mattresses, linen sheets and warm
blankets made them very comfortable. Heavy curtains surrounded
the beds, for the Elizabethans disliked draughts. Each night after
they retired, their servants would carefully pull the curtains and
shut them in, safe and secure from any whiff of fresh air!

FLOOR-COVERINGS   Rather surprisingly, with all their riches,
the wealthy Elizabethans did not normally have carpets on the
floor. At this time carpets were so expensive that they were used
to cover beds and tables. Rushes were strewn on the floor, and
these soon became so dirty that fleas made their homes there.
Tusser, a writer of the time, advised his countrymen to use a
sweet-smelling herb, for, as he said:

"Where chamber is swept and wormwood is strown,
No flea for his life dare abide to be known".

CONCLUSION   Despite their lack of carpets, bathrooms or
running water, which we now consider a necessity, these Elizabethan mansions were certainly magnificent homes. They, together with the country houses and all the splendours of London
and the other towns, showed clearly that England was fast leaving
the Middle Ages and advancing towards the Modern Age.

3 · *The Elizabethans*

IMPRESSIVE as were the towns, cities and mansions of Elizabethan England, their appearance could not match that of the people. The Elizabethans loved to wear gay, colourful garments of fine silk and velvet, and they often looked most striking. Rich men were dressed in yellow or white silk stockings, velvet trunks or trunk hose, and purple, green or orange padded doublets embroidered with gold and with lace at the wrists. They often wore a short dark cloak attached to the shoulders of the doublet. Ladies wore long satin dresses which had pointed, narrow waists and underneath a farthingale of whalebone or leather to hold the skirts out stiffly. Their sleeves were edged with lace, and large white ruffs or collars jutted out from their necks. Men, too, wore ruffs, and if they were unlucky enough to be caught in the rain "their great ruffes would strike sayle and flutter like dishe-clouts about their necks". The clothes of the children differed little from those of their parents, for the Elizabethans tended to regard children as smaller versions of themselves.

Only the rich could afford to dress as well as this. Poor people had to be content with clothes of black or brown linen and rough wool. Some spent much more money than they could afford on clothes, and apprentices were notorious for squandering all their wages on silk stockings and embroidered shirts. The authorities tried to make them behave more sensibly and ordered them to dress in a "small plain slop" (a loose smock or gown) and a flat woollen cap. Any apprentice who disobeyed and appeared on the streets in his finery could be punished with a whipping.

HAIR-STYLES   The hair-styles of the Elizabethans were often just as eye-catching as their clothes. Ladies sometimes dressed their hair in fantastic shapes which they propped up with wire. Many dyed their hair, and others, like the Queen, wore wigs. For a time red hair was fashionable, but later gold or blonde hair became all the rage. Hair was dyed with gold dust, and wigs were obtained by buying the locks of golden-haired children for 1d. Ladies also liked to have long eyebrows and eyelashes, and to make them grow they applied a paste made from "young mice beaten into small pieces and mixed with old wine".

Men, too, tried to keep in the fashion. Some wore their hair long at the ears and curled in the Spanish style. Others adopted the French fashion with a "love-lock" dropping to the shoulders, or the Italian, where the hair was short and round like a half moon. Beards might be shaped like a spade or pointed, while moustaches were sometimes laid out from one cheek to another and turned up like two horns.

COSMETICS AND PERFUMES   In their effort to look as attractive as possible, Elizabethan women rouged and powdered their
faces heavily. Both men and women used perfumes like civet,
musk and oil of tartar, perhaps because they were not very fond of
washing. One writer of the time was tremendously impressed by
the fact that the Queen had a "bath every three months whether
she needed it or not".

DIET   The Elizabethans also paid great attention to their food.
The poorer people grew cucumbers, radishes, pumpkins, carrots
and turnips to add variety to the traditional diet of beans, bacon,
milk, curds, and ale or cider. The rich bought costly wines from
the Continent, and they were continually trying out new delicacies
such as caviarre from Russia. But some people were rather
suspicious of the new foods, and one squire when he received a
barrel of caviarre from a friend returned it with a note saying:
"Commend me to my lady, but tell her we have black soap
enough already".

BANQUETS   Wealthy Elizabethans loved to invite their friends
to great banquets where they could show off their latest fare.
There would be five or six courses, and the food was served on
plates of silver and the wines drunk from the finest glassware. But
eating habits were not much better than those of the poor people
with their wooden bowls and platters. There were no forks, and
people either scooped up their food with a spoon or "speared it
with a sharp-pointed knife and so popped it into the mouth".

    Entertainments at banquets were also quite boisterous. The
Elizabethans loved practical jokes, and often the host would arrange
a custard splashing. A huge bowl of custard was placed on the

table for dessert, and then a small boy would leap into it and splash about. All the guests in their finest clothes would be covered in custard; though they knew what was going to happen, and had seen it countless times before, they all thought it was wonderful fun.

ENTERTAINMENTS   After the guests finished their meal, the host might entertain them with a masque. This was a short play with music, dancing and poetry, and normally some of the guests would be the actors. After the masque there would be dancing, for this was the favourite pastime of almost everyone in Elizabethan England. The upper classes liked the stately and gracious "pavane", the lively "galliard", or the "volta" in which the dancers whirled around and then leapt up in the air. The ordinary people preferred to dance jigs, hornpipes and morris dances.

SOME ELIZABETHAN RECIPES

TO DRESS A CRABBE   First take away all the legges (and the heades) and then take the fishe out of the shell. Put the meate into a dishe and butter it upon a chafing-dish or coales. And put to them cinnamon and sugar and a little vinegar. When you have chafed it season it and put the meat into the shell againe.

TO BOILE SPARROWS   Take two ladles full of mutton broth and a little whole mace, put in a peece of sweet butter and a handful of parsly, season it with sugar verjuice and a little pepper.

TO BOILE PIGEONS WITH RICE   Boyle them in mutton broth, putting sweete herbes in their bellies. Then take a little rice and boile it in creame with a little whole mace. Season it with sugar. Lay it thick on their breasts, wringing the juice of a lemon upon them, and so serve.

Viol, virginal and hautboy

MUSIC   The Elizabethans were also very fond of music, and often had musical evenings in their homes. They would sing madrigals or part songs, and play musical instruments like the viol, the violon, the recorder, cornet, hautboy, virginal, organ and flute. At this time there were several fine composers such as William Byrd, Orlando Gibbons and John Dow, and the madrigals which they composed are still frequently performed. The most popular musical instrument was the flute, and often flutes were to be found lying in a barber's shop for the customers to use.

RECREATIONS   On evenings when they were not singing or dancing, the Elizabethans might play games like cards, draughts, chess, backgammon, shovel board, ninepins or shuttlecock. They also loved stories read from books describing strange places and animals. One of their favourite books was Pliny's "The Secrets and Wonders of the World", and they would sit for hours listening to tales of dogs that had "hands and feet like men", and of fishes that at night "come out of the sea".

Much as they liked listening to stories, the Elizabethans preferred to be out in the open air whenever possible. The upper classes spent a great deal of time hawking, hunting, playing games like bowls, pall-mall and skittles, or practising archery and rapier fencing. Those who attended the Queen's Court sometimes played a kind of tennis.

The games and sports of the ordinary people were often very rough. Two of their favourite sports were wrestling and cudgel play, a contest where the opponents attempted to strike each other on the head with a long pole. They also played a kind of football which was more like a pitched battle than a game. Two teams of any number lined up on some suitable piece of ground and then tried to force the ball towards the wall or gate that was their opponents' goal. Injuries were common, and one Elizabethan writer described how sometimes "their necks are broken, sometimes their backs, sometimes their legs, sometimes their arms; . . . sometimes their noses gush out their blood".

FAIRS AND FESTIVALS   At Easter, Whitsuntide, Christmas and all the other festivals the Elizabethans held special celebrations. There was dancing and feasting, cock-fighting, sports, and perhaps a great football match between two rival villages. Most districts also had a fair two or three times a year, and then the people were able to see jugglers, acrobats and many kinds of side-shows.

CHILDREN'S GAMES   Children in Elizabethan times would normally watch or take part in the sports and entertainments provided for the adults, but they also had their own amusements. Small children had dolls and toy soldiers, while their older brothers and sisters played with marbles, skipping ropes, balloons, stilts, tops, hoops, and kites. Some of their favourite games were skittles, shuttlecock, bat and ball, and cup and ball.

EDUCATION   The lives of children at this time was not all play, however, for from an early age they were expected to do all sorts of odd jobs to help their parents. Few of them attended school, for only rarely were there schools in the villages and country districts. Even in the towns it was normally only the sons of rich parents who went to school. Girls did not attend school, but if their parents were rich they might be educated at home by private tutors. The sons of wealthy parents who lived in the country were also taught by private tutors.

Those boys fortunate enough to live near a town and whose parents could afford the fees would go first of all to a preparatory school. Then when they had learnt to read and write they would move on to a grammar school. These schools were founded especially to teach Latin grammar, which is the reason for their name. Almost all of the larger towns had a grammar school, and during Elizabeth's reign many new schools such as Repton, Merchant Taylors, Rugby, Uppingham and Harrow were founded. At the age of fifteen a clever boy might pass from Grammar School to University at Oxford or Cambridge. Poor boys did sometimes manage to go to University, as they could pay their way by working for their wealthier fellow students.

THE GRAMMAR SCHOOL Often pupils in the grammar schools were forbidden to talk English so that their Latin would be improved. They also worked much harder than modern pupils. Their schoolday began with prayers at six in the morning, and lessons continued till six in the evening, with only a short break for lunch and brief intervals in the morning and afternoon. The pupils had a half-holiday on Thursdays, but they worked all day on Saturdays, and on Sundays and Holy Days they attended church with their masters. Their only holidays were twelve days at Easter, nine at Whitsuntide and eighteen at Christmas.

Schoolmasters in Elizabethan times were far sterner than modern teachers. A writer of the time tells us that boys "were whipped and scourged and beat" until "from top to toe the skin is away".

SUPERSTITIONS AND WITCHCRAFT Since few of the Elizabethans were really educated, we need not be too surprised to find that most men and women were very superstitious. They believed in fairies, elves and goblins, wore charms, and often recited spells to ward off evil fortune or to bring them good luck. They frequently visited astrologers who told them their fortunes and fates from the movements of the stars. Many human beings, it was claimed, had magical powers. Some were alchemists who could change ordinary metals into gold, some were sorcerers who could cast spells on people, and others were witches who had made a compact with the Devil in return for all sorts of strange powers.

The Elizabethans were so terrified of witchcraft that any woman suspected of being a witch was either imprisoned or put to death, according to her offence. And often it did not require very much evidence to have a woman condemned. If she was old, seemed rather odd and was cross with her neighbours, people would begin to look suspiciously at her. Then if some misfortune occurred in the village, everyone would begin to whisper that she had caused it. One man related how an old woman had been very angry with him when he refused to give her some milk. "She cursed me," he declared, "and soon afterwards my child, my cow, my sow and my pullet died." Everyone believed that the old woman had been responsible, and the unfortunate wretch was executed.

REMEDIES AND MEDICINES   In their treatment of illness and disease, too, the Elizabethans were often very superstitious. Many people, for instance, believed that headaches would disappear if only the sufferer would place a "halter round his neck wherewith one has been hanged". There were indeed doctors, physicians and tooth-pullers, but doctors treated almost every complaint with blood-letting, while physicians and tooth-pullers carried out their operations without anaesthetics. There were also herbalists and apothecaries who sold drugs and cures, but most of their cures were foul-tasting and loathsome concoctions. Yet sometimes it did happen that the strange ideas of the Elizabethans had real medical value. Thus they were accustomed to hang red cloth over the windows when someone was suffering from smallpox. For a long time this seemed a mere superstition, but doctors now know that red articles filter out the rays of the sun which cause scarring in smallpox patients.

PLAGUE   Smallpox was one of the most dreaded diseases in Elizabethan times, but the plague was feared even more. Its victims suffered from a high fever and racking pains, and then their bodies turned black. The people living in the towns were particularly in danger, and during one attack in London in 1592 over 20,000 people died. Here is a description of the grim conditions written by an Elizabethan, Thomas Dekker:

"The plague, having beaten many thousands of men, women and children to death, is the cause that all the inhabitants walk up and down like mourners at some funeral. The poison of this infection strikes so deep into all men's hearts that their cheeks have lost their colours. All merry meetings are cut off, all assemblies dissolved; mirth is departed and lies dead and buried in men's bosoms."

The plague was spread by fleas carried by rats, and the Elizabethans had no cure. They believed that stray dogs carried the disease, and so they killed the very animals that might have cut down the numbers of rats. The disease therefore raged unchecked and many of the people fled from the town into the surrounding countryside. But often they carried the plague with them, and large numbers died in the fields, woods and ditches.

Yet even during the worst epidemics, the Elizabethans never gave way to despair. Though many people fled from the towns, even more stayed behind and carried on as best they could. In their own way they were just as brave as any of the adventurers on the high seas, for the enemy they had to face was the most powerful and fearful imaginable. And when the attack was over, they quickly resumed their normal lives with all their customary zest and energy. Nothing, not even the terrors of the plague, could permanently dampen the spirits of the Elizabethans.

4 · *Government and Defence*

THE men and women of Elizabethan England were certainly a most impressive people in every way, but without doubt the outstanding personality of the Age was the Queen herself. Daughter of the stout and jovial King Henry VIII, she was as gay, colourful and courageous as any of her subjects, and also a woman of tremendous ability. She could speak seven languages fluently, was an accomplished musician, and had a lively interest in painting, poetry and many other subjects. Elizabeth was a brilliant ruler, and often in negotiations she could outwit the best statesmen of the day. She was also an excellent judge of character, and able to choose loyal and talented men to serve her.

It was fortunate for England that Elizabeth was such a gifted woman, for in the sixteenth century the King or Queen was the real ruler of the country. There was no Cabinet or Prime Minister, and it was the Queen who took all the important decisions. She did have a small council of ministers to assist her, but it was always the Queen who finally decided what the policies of the country should be. One of the most famous of her councillors was Sir William Cecil, an ancestor of the present Lord Salisbury.

THE COURT   Most of the work of the government was carried on in the Queen's Palace at Whitehall. She had a small room known as the Privy Chamber where she discussed government business with her councillors. There were also several Presence Chambers, and in these she received ambassadors, nobles and ambitious young men who wished to obtain employment.

But the Queen's Palace was not merely a place of business. This was the home of the Queen, and here she loved to relax and be gay among the lords and ladies who lived at Court. On many evenings there was dancing, and the Queen and her courtiers would enjoy themselves thoroughly. "The dancers danced behind one another," wrote a foreign visitor who had attended the Court, "and they all wore gloves. While dancing they often curtsied to one another. Slender and beautiful were the women and magnificently robed. Meanwhile the Queen chatted and jested most amiably with young and old. Pointing her finger at one gentleman she told him there was a smut on his face. She offered to wipe it off with her handkerchief but he removed it himself."

PROGRESSES   Much as she loved her Court at Whitehall, Elizabeth left it frequently to go on tours or progresses. Each year she visited a different part of the country so that she could see her people and they could see their Queen. Often she rode on horseback, and large crowds lined the route to see her pass. Elizabeth enjoyed these progresses, and she took great pleasure in the shouts and cheers of her subjects. Even when she was growing old she would not abandon them, and as late as 1601 at the age of sixty-seven she set out once more. "Let the old stay behind and the young and able go," she declared when some of her ministers complained and grumbled.

PARLIAMENT   Although Elizabeth herself was the real ruler of the country, England did have a Parliament in the sixteenth century. It was much weaker than the modern Parliament, however, and met only when summoned by the Queen. Towards the end of Elizabeth's reign Parliament began to increase its powers,

The Queen on a progress

and in the following reigns of James I and Charles I it was to become strong enough to defy the King. In 1642 it was even able to organise a Civil War against Charles I.

RELIGION   In the same way that she was head of the government, Elizabeth also ruled over the Church. Her father, Henry VIII, had refused to accept the Pope in Rome as head of the Church and had made himself head of the Church in England. Her sister, Mary, later restored England to the Roman Catholic Church, but in 1559 Elizabeth established a new English Church with herself as Supreme Governor. She had bishops and archbishops appointed to govern the Church's affairs, but she made quite certain that her own wishes were carried out.

Everyone in England was by law compelled to attend the services of Elizabeth's Church. Any person who was absent from Sunday worship could be fined 1s.! Some people, however, remained faithful Roman Catholics, and instead of obeying the law they went to services held by priests in secret. The government then began to persecute them and any priests who were caught celebrating mass were arrested and executed; but still a small

number refused to accept the new Church. Another group who would not obey the Queen were the Puritans. These were extreme Protestants who wished to abolish bishops and to make Church services "pure" and simple, and free from splendour and ritual. They, too, were persecuted, and several of the leaders were put to death.

LOCAL GOVERNMENT   Although Elizabeth was the ruler of the government and of the Church, she did not have very much control over local affairs. Most towns were ruled by a small council of wealthy citizens. Normally there were no elections, and when one councillor died the other members would merely appoint someone else in his place. In country districts much of the work of government was carried on by landowners who had been appointed to the position of Justice of the Peace.

Frame pillory, stocks *and 'stretch-neck' pillory*

LAW AND ORDER   One of the duties of the councils and the Justices of the Peace was to maintain law and order. They appointed some of the local citizens or villagers as constables, but these were only part-time officials and they received no pay. In the towns there was also a small body of men known as the watch whose duty it was to patrol the streets. Neither the watch nor the constables were very efficient, and most criminals escaped capture. The government therefore tried to prevent crime by imposing severe penalties on those who were unfortunate enough to be caught, to act as a warning to all the others. For minor offences men might be flogged or put in the stocks or pillory, while for many crimes including robbery the punishment was death. Punishments were carried out in public, and huge crowds turned out to see criminals executed.

"THE STURDY BEGGARS"   One of the most serious problems that faced the authorities in Elizabethan England was the tremendous increase in unemployment in country districts. Many men had lost their lands when sheep-farming was introduced, for this type of farming required far fewer workers than the raising of crops. They began to move around the country looking for work, but often there was none to be found.

To make a living for themselves and their families, some of the unemployed became minstrels, fortune-tellers, jugglers, pedlars or hawkers. Others became expert beggars and thought up all sorts of tricks to make people part with their money. They covered their limbs with sores to rouse sympathy, they placed soap in their mouths and pretended they had the falling sickness, or they acted as if they were mad.

When they could not obtain enough money by begging, many men began stealing. Some known as "Anglers" used long poles to "fish" clothes from hedges, while others called "Priggers" stole horses from fields. Sometimes whole gangs of these ruffians would work together under a leader called the Upright Man. Normally he was a fierce, violent fellow, and he collected a portion of all the money taken or stolen by the members of the gang.

Not content with such minor crimes, many vagabonds turned to highway robbery. So numerous did the highwaymen become that several roads were quite infested with them. Travellers could seldom journey past such areas as Gadshill near Rochester, Salisbury Plain, and Newmarket Heath without being attacked. Many innkeepers were in league with them and passed on information about wealthy travellers who were staying at their inns.

The government was exceedingly alarmed. It tried to stamp out the highwaymen by ensuring that anyone convicted of this crime was executed. It also dealt harshly with the beggars and passed laws declaring that any able-bodied person over fourteen who was convicted of begging was to be "grievously whipped and burnt through the gristle of the right ear with a hot iron of the compass of an inch about". If a man persisted in begging after this and was arrested a third time, then he might be sentenced to death. The sick, the disabled and the old, however, were given permission to beg, and each parish was ordered to raise rates to provide assistance for them.

Over the years the measures taken by the government were reasonably successful. The sick and the disabled were provided for, and the numbers of highwaymen, robbers and able-bodied beggars were cut down by the harsh punishments imposed. Sometimes, too, the authorities thought up new ideas to discourage men from begging. In London large numbers of beggars were rounded up and forced to clean out the filthy ditches in the city. Such treatment made the beggars keep well away from the city, for, as one justice wrote, they would rather "hazard their lives than work".

DEFENCE: THE ARMY   In the same way that the police forces were not very efficient in Elizabethan times, so, too, the defence forces of the nation were far from perfect. There was no regular army, but only a militia which could be called upon in times of emergency. Each county contributed a certain number of men, but these were rarely the best soldiers in the district. Rich men bribed the captains to choose someone else, while Justices of the Peace often made sure that only troublemakers and those who were unfit to work in the fields were chosen.

Clearly the army raised by such means could not be expected to

A highwayman advancing on a rich traveller

fight very well in battle, but fortunately the situation improved later in Elizabeth's reign. More care was taken with the training of the militia, and gradually the military standards were raised. Some counties gained a better reputation than others, and Somerset in particular became noted for the number and quality of its troops.

Many Englishmen also gained military experience fighting with the Dutch in their struggle for independence against the Spaniards. They soon showed that they were a match for the Spanish infantry, then the finest soldiers in Europe. Thus if England were threatened with attack these veteran soldiers could quickly return home to become the officers and the leaders of the defence militia in England.

SIR PHILIP SIDNEY   One of the most famous of all the soldiers in Queen Elizabeth's reign was Sir Philip Sidney. He was born in Kent in 1554, and as a young man he travelled in many countries on the Continent. He tried to join Drake and Raleigh on some of their early expeditions, but something always turned up to prevent his going. Then in 1585 he went with an English army to the Netherlands to help the Dutch rebels. He soon proved himself an excellent officer, and he performed many deeds of valour. But in 1586 he was wounded when leading an attack, and a few days later he died. As he was lying wounded, he was offered a drink, but Sir Philip's first thought was not for himself, but for his men. Though he was parched with thirst, he refused to take any of the water and passed the water bottle on to a wounded soldier lying beside him.

THE NAVY   Despite the bravery and courage of such men as Sir Philip Sidney, the main defence of England at this time lay in its fighting ships. During Elizabeth's reign, many individuals like Drake and Hawkins had built armed vessels to sail on raids against the Spaniards, and these could quickly be formed into large and powerful fleets if England were attacked. There were also thousands of highly skilled seamen to man these ships—seamen who had fought and won in numerous battles and engagements against the Spaniards in the New World.

England had also a small regular navy. When Elizabeth came to the throne in 1558, there had been few seaworthy vessels, but gradually several new ships were built and old ones re-fitted. There was a great improvement in the design of the new ships, and they became faster and more manoeuvrable. By 1603 there were twenty-nine ships in the navy, and these together with the ships owned by private individuals could make up a formidable force.

The most important fighting ship in the Elizabethan navy was the galleon. This was a three- or four-masted sailing ship with one or two covered decks and a raised poop and forecastle. Heavy guns were placed along the sides of the ship on the covered decks, and these fired through portholes that could be closed with wooden shutters. One of the most powerful of the Elizabethan galleons was the 690-ton *Ark Royal* built in 1587. She carried thirty-two guns and had a crew of 270 men.

'Ark Royal'

5 · Dangers and Alarms

ALTHOUGH England's army and navy were growing steadily stronger in the late sixteenth century, the country was continually threatened with attack and invasion for almost the whole of Elizabeth's reign. The great Roman Catholic Powers of France and Spain were a constant menace, and there was always the possibility that they would try to restore England to the Catholic Church by force. Nor was Elizabeth's own position at all secure. The Roman Catholics in England disliked having a Protestant Queen, and many of them were involved in plots to get rid of her.

MARY QUEEN OF SCOTS   One of the greatest dangers to Elizabeth came from her cousin, Mary Queen of Scots. Mary was a Roman Catholic, and, as she was a descendant of Henry VII, she was regarded by many English Catholics as the rightful ruler of the country. For the first few years of her reign Elizabeth was continually afraid that Mary might lead an attack against her from Scotland—perhaps with the aid of French or Spanish troops.

Then in 1567 civil war broke out in Scotland. Mary was forced to flee across the Border to England, and her infant son was proclaimed King by the Protestant lords who now ruled Scotland. Elizabeth at once had Mary imprisoned, for she feared that the English Catholics might rise in revolt to support her.

Yet even as a prisoner Mary continued to prove a threat to the English Queen. In 1570 the Pope excommunicated Elizabeth and declared her deposed. Soon many plots were being organised to assassinate Elizabeth and to put Mary on the throne. Elizabeth tried to stop them by passing harsh laws against the Catholics and having Mary guarded more closely, but the conspiracies continued throughout the nineteen long years Mary remained a prisoner in England.

After some time, Elizabeth and her ministers decided that they must take even more drastic action. They laid a trap for Mary by tricking her into believing that a foolproof method had been found of passing messages between herself and her supporters. She wrapped her notes in a waterproof case and then placed the case in an empty beer barrel. The barrel was taken out of her prison, the notes were delivered to her friends, and then their answers were brought back in a full beer barrel shortly afterwards. But unfortunately for Mary, Elizabeth's spies knew all about the scheme and could intercept the barrels. The notes were copied out and read by government ministers before being passed on to Mary or to her fellow-conspirators.

Mary in prison

Soon the government learnt of a new plot to assassinate Elizabeth. The conspirators were arrested and executed, and then Mary was tried for treason. Mary protested that as a Scottish Queen she could not possibly be a traitor in England, but nevertheless she was found guilty of plotting Elizabeth's death. On 8 February 1587 she was executed in the Great Hall at Fotheringay castle in Northamptonshire.

Mary met her death with true queenly grace and courage. She was dressed in robes of the finest black satin, and on her head she wore a pointed cap over an auburn periwig. She carried a crucifix, a prayer book and a chain of scented beads with her to the scaffold. At no time did she show the slightest sign of fear, and she acted with regal courtesy to the officials and the executioner. On the scaffold she made her last speech, and then said her prayers, asking God to forgive her enemies and those who were responsible for her death. When she had finished, her eyes were bandaged with a gold embroidered veil and she was led to the block. Once more she made a short prayer, and then the executioner's axe descended on her neck.

Yet hardly had the danger from Mary Queen of Scots been removed than Elizabeth was faced with the prospect of a Spanish invasion. King Philip of Spain had many reasons for making war on England. English sailors were continually attacking his colonies and treasure ships, while English soldiers were aiding the Dutch rebels. Then, as the greatest Catholic monarch in Europe, he often dreamed of conquering Protestant England and making it Catholic once more. For a time he held back, but when Mary Queen of Scots was executed and left him her claims to the English throne, Philip decided that the time had come to invade England.

THE ARMADA   Soon the shipyards of Spain were working feverishly to build a great fleet. The preparations were delayed when in 1587 Drake sailed boldly into Cadiz harbour and destroyed many half-finished ships; but the Spaniards soon made good these losses. By the summer of 1588 everything was ready, and on 12 July a great Armada of 130 ships set sail for the Netherlands to embark a powerful Spanish army stationed there. This army was then to be landed on the south coast of England, together with the soldiers carried on the ships from Spain.

On 29 July news was carried to England that the Armada had been sighted off Lizard Point in Cornwall. Most people were exceedingly alarmed, but the naval commanders and their men were supremely confident. Drake, we are told, even finished his game of bowls before he and the other captains boarded their ships to sail them out of Plymouth.

Once they were clear of the harbour, the English ships took up a position to windward and to the rear of the Armada. From there they began to launch frequent attacks against the Spanish ships. Yet though they inflicted much damage and caused many casualties, they were unable to break up the great crescent-shaped formation that the Spaniards had made as they moved steadily up Channel.

FIRESHIPS   Passing on through the Channel, the Armada anchored off the French coast at Calais. This was a serious blunder. At midnight on 6 August the English commanders sent eight fireships drifting on the tide towards the Spanish vessels. The Spaniards were terror-stricken. "They came towards us all in flames," wrote a Spanish officer. "One of them flared up with such fierceness and great noise as were frightful; the ships of the Armada cut their cables, leaving their anchors and running out to sea."

51

GRAVELINES   In the confusion that followed the Spanish ships scattered in all directions. The following morning English vessels once more moved into the attack off Gravelines. After a fierce battle, victory went to the English fleet, and the surviving Spaniards were driven into the North Sea.

Many people throughout Europe had thought that the Armada was invincible, but in actual fact it was much less powerful than it seemed. The Spaniards still fought in an old-fashioned way and their main aim in a battle was to get to close quarters and board the enemy ships. The English fleet was comparatively modern. Its ships could fight at a distance since they carried more guns, and these were mounted in such a way that they could fire broadsides. English ships were also far more manoeuvrable than the larger, rather clumsy Spanish galleons.

At Gravelines the ships of the Armada had suffered severely, and the Spaniards had no desire to face the English fleet again in battle. They therefore decided to sail north round Scotland and so home to Spain. But many of the Spanish ships were so badly damaged that some foundered in the Atlantic storms and others were driven ashore on the west coasts of Scotland and Ireland. Only a very small number of battered ships managed at length to reach Spain, and most were full of sick and wounded men.

THE "REVENGE"   Yet despite the great English victory, the war with Spain dragged on for many years. In 1591 there occurred one of the most memorable and brave actions in naval history. Off the Azores, a small group of islands in the Atlantic, the *Revenge* commanded by Sir Richard Grenville was trapped and surrounded by fifty-three Spanish galleons. For twenty-four hours the gallant English ship was pounded by the Spaniards. Attack after attack

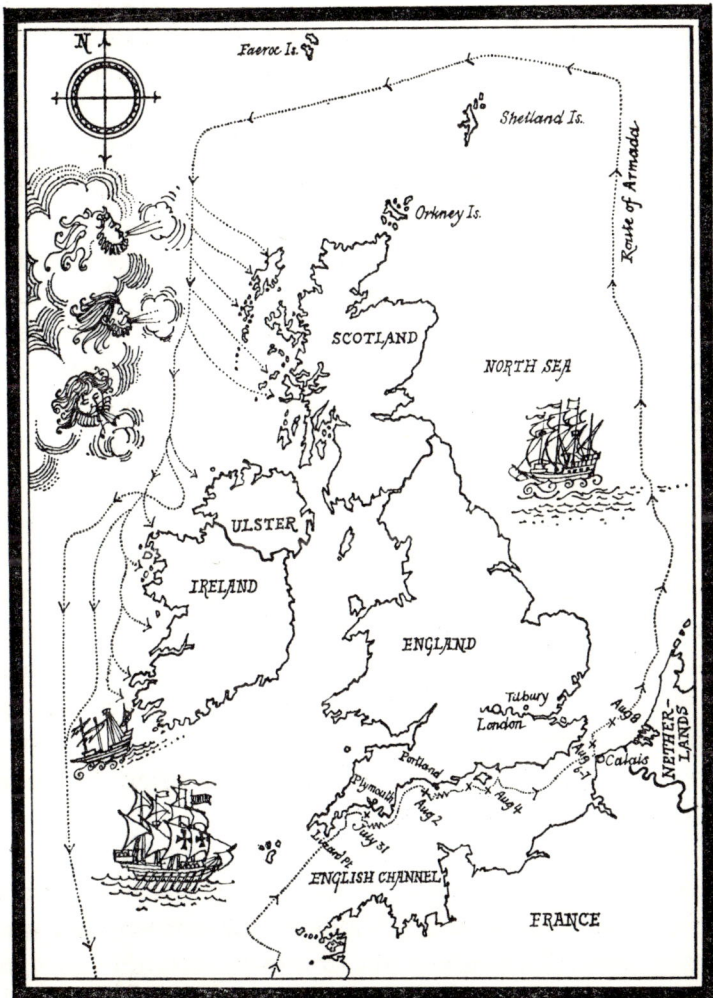

Faeroe Is.

Shetland Is.

Orkney Is.

Route of Armada

SCOTLAND

NORTH SEA

ULSTER

IRELAND

ENGLAND

Tilbury
London

NETHERLANDS

Calais
Aug 8

Portland
Plymouth
July 31
Aug 2
Aug 4

ENGLISH CHANNEL

FRANCE

was beaten back. But at last, with his ship almost a total wreck and most of his crew already dead, Sir Richard surrendered. Shortly afterwards he died of his wounds, but among all seafaring men his indomitable courage will always be remembered.

IRELAND   During the war, the Spaniards tried to make trouble for England in her colony of Ireland. The Irish had always resented English rule. After the Reformation they became even more discontented, for while England had become a Protestant country, most of the Irish remained loyal to the Pope. They broke out in frequent rebellions during Elizabeth's reign, and Spanish troops and advisers landed in Ireland to assist them. The English government feared that Ireland might become a base for an attack on England, so they crushed the rebellions very severely; but this merely made the Irish more bitter than ever.

In an effort to overcome the Irish resistance, Elizabeth and her ministers decided to send settlers over to Ireland to form a core of loyal and peaceful subjects. They were given the lands taken from Irish rebels, and later in the reign of James I more settlers from England and Scotland were sent out to Ulster in the north. But the Irish resented losing their lands and a sharp division appeared between the settlers and the native Irish. From this has arisen the modern partition of Ireland into Northern Ireland and the Republic of Ireland.

Obviously, Elizabeth's government had not found a final answer to the Irish problem. It did manage to put down the rebellions, but the Irish people's longing for independence was as strong as ever. Throughout the following centuries they rose against their conquerors time after time until at last in 1922 they won the right to govern themselves.

Elizabeth addressing her troops at Tilbury

"GLORIANA"   Yet despite the continued uprisings in Ireland,
Elizabeth was certainly much more secure in the final years of her
reign than at her coronation in 1558. The defeat of the Armada
and the execution of Mary Queen of Scots had removed the worst
risks. The danger from the Roman Catholics, too, proved much
less than in earlier years, for many of them had fought gallantly
against the Armada and not on the side of the Spaniards as had
been feared.

The people of England firmly believed that the Queen herself had brought them safely through all the perils surrounding them. Even in the darkest days she had never despaired, and, as the Armada sailed towards England, she inspired the whole nation by riding out to Tilbury and addressing her troops:

> "I know I have the body of a weak and feeble woman, but I have the heart and stomach of a king, and of a king of England, too, and think foul scorn that Spain or any prince of Europe should dare to invade the borders of my realm. I know by your valour we shall shortly have a famous victory over those enemies of my God, of my kingdom, and my people".

Elizabeth rightly deserved the reverence and honour which her people showed in the closing years of her reign. She had first of all won their admiration by her courage and her outstanding gift of leadership. Then as each year passed, their respect deepened into love and devotion, until at last she became their own "Good Queen Bess", their "Gloriana".

6 · *A Golden Age*

THE years after the defeat of the Armada in 1588 were a wonderful period for the Elizabethans. Their great victory had won them the admiration of all Europe, and they were brimming over with confidence. They felt that they were the greatest nation on earth, ruled by the greatest Queen of all times.

But as the years passed, some people began to look anxiously towards the future. They could see that the Queen was growing old, and they wondered if England would continue to win such glory when she was gone. And since Elizabeth refused to name her successor, they became even more fearful about what would happen after her death.

DEATH OF DRAKE AND HAWKINS   The feeling that a Golden Age was passing away was intensified by the deaths of two of the most famous Elizabethans. In 1596 Drake and Hawkins set out on what proved to be their last expedition to the New World. Hawkins died on the voyage, and Drake died of dysentery near Nombre de Dios. The loss of these heroes cast a gloom over the hearts of many in England.

DEATH OF QUEEN ELIZABETH   When in 1603 Elizabeth grew ill and died, and a horseman galloped north to offer the Crown to James of Scotland, England sorrowfully mourned both their Queen and the passing of "the good old days". They knew within themselves that the future would be much duller. The Queen had for a time brought glory and romance to their lives, and now they realised they must live like ordinary mortals again.

SEA-POWER   Yet if the Elizabethan Age was over, the achievements of those memorable years did not disappear. England still retained the command of the seas she had won in the Channel and the oceans of the New World, and for long centuries the heirs of Drake and Hawkins continued to patrol the coasts of their nation. Other rulers like Louis XIV of France, Napoleon, the Kaiser of Germany, and Hitler would threaten to conquer Britain; but always her navy and her seamen would be there to defeat their plans.

EMPIRE   The first attempts by Raleigh and the other colonists to create an Empire were not forgotten. In the following reign more successful colonies were established, and so began a great Empire that was eventually to cover a very large part of the world. The Elizabethans had not foreseen the exciting expansion of the future but they had been the true pioneers of the British Empire.

The Elizabethans have been a lasting inspiration to all the generations that have come after them. Men and women have continually thrilled to hear and read about the deeds and exploits of Drake, Hawkins, Raleigh, Shakespeare and the Queen. When faced with danger they have endeavoured to follow the example of their brave countrymen.

Nor is it only the names of the heroes and leaders that shine out through the ages, for the ordinary Elizabethans, too, seem to have a glory and a glamour that wins our admiration. Perhaps what is so attractive about them is their zest for life. They were never dull and gloomy, and all that they did they tackled with eagerness and enjoyment. Whether they were sailing to the Isthmus of Panama or going to a play, whether they were sailing in the seas of the Arctic or visiting London, they did it all with tremendous

Raleigh smoking tobacco

enthusiasm. When they faced dangers, they seemed to enjoy rather than fear them.

There was a darker side to the Elizabethans, however, which we cannot find attractive. They were often self-seeking, and many of them, including Drake, were determined to win a fortune no matter what it might cost other people. Some of their sports were very cruel, and the punishments inflicted on wrongdoers were often savage and barbaric. Nor did the Elizabethans seem to see anything wrong in slavery, and they were quite prepared to transport and sell African slaves to the Spaniards in the New World.

Yet with all their faults and vices, the Elizabethans were a truly splendid people. They wrote enthralling plays and composed beautiful music. They faced great dangers with calm courage, and they defeated strong and powerful enemies. Above all they were prepared to adventure into unknown seas seeking new trade routes and carrying the English flag to every corner of the world. Though their fathers had hardly ever left their villages, the Elizabethans roamed the whole world. And whereas their fathers had been interested only in the affairs of their farms and local markets, now there was knowledgeable talk of the West Indies, the Pacific, the North-West Passage and the Strait of Magellan.

We today have clearly much to learn from the Elizabethans. If somehow we could recapture their zestful spirit of adventure and their gaiety, then we would certainly be more able to deal with the tasks that face us. Avoiding the cruelties and selfishness that sometimes marred the achievements of the Elizabethans we might then go forward to create a second Elizabethan Age where the men and women of all countries could live full, adventurous and satisfying lives.

Time Chart

	EVENTS IN ENGLAND	EVENTS OVERSEAS
1550		First attempt to find a N.E. Passage
	Elizabeth becomes Queen Elizabethan Church Settlement	Anthony Jenkinson sets out for Persia
1560		First voyage of John Hawkins to New World
	Mary Queen of Scots flees to England	Spaniards attack Hawkins' ships
1570	Pope excommunicates Elizabeth	
		Drake ambushes the mule train
		Frobisher attempts to find the N.W. Passage
		Drake's voyage round the World
1580	Drake knighted	
		First settlement in Newfoundland
		Raleigh establishes colony of Virginia Death of Sir Philip Sidney
	Execution of Mary Queen of Scots	Raleigh's second settlement
		The Armada
1590	London stricken with the plague	Last fight of the 'Revenge'
		Death of Drake and Hawkins
1600		East India Company founded
	Death of Queen Elizabeth	
1610		

Books to Read

Andrist, R. K. *Heroes of Polar Exploration* (Cassell, Caravel Series)

Allan, A. B. *The Spacious Days of Queen Elizabeth* (Barrie and Rockcliff, New Project History Series)

Brown, I. *Shakespeare* (Collins)

Byrne, M. St. C. *Elizabethan Life in Town and Country* (Methuen)

Cammiade, A. *Elizabeth the First* (Methuen)

Dawlish, P. *Young Drake of Devon* (Oxford University Press)

Dawlish, P. *Martin Frobisher* (Oxford University Press)

Dodd, A. H. *Life in Elizabethan England* (Batsford, English Life Series)

France, C. G. *Discovering Sailing Ships* (University of London Press)

Irwin, M. *Young Bess* (Chatto and Windus)

Lewis, M. *Histroy of the British Navy* (Allen and Unwin)

Nicoll, A. *The Elizabethans* (Cambridge University Press)

Quennell, M. & C. H. B. *Everyday Things in England, 1500–1799* (Batsford)

Taylor, D. *The Elizabethan Age* (Dobson, Living in England Series)

Trease, G. *Fortune my Foe: Sir Walter Raleigh* (Methuen)

Wright, L. B. *Shakespeare's England* (Cassell, Caravel Series)

NOVELS

Chute, M. *The Wonderful Winter* (Harrap)

Dawlish, P. *He Went With Drake* (Oxford University Press)

Harnett, C. *Stars of Fortune* (Methuen)

Ross, S. *A Masque of Traitors* (Hodder)

Scott, Sir Walter *Kenilworth* (Collins)

Sutcliff, R. *The Armourer's House* (Oxford University Press)

Sutcliff, R. *The Queen Elizabeth Story* (Oxford University Press)

Wibberley, L. *The King's Beard* (Faber)

Index

houses, London, 19; country houses, 24;
    mansions, 24–6

inns, 21, 43
industries, 23
Ireland, 54, 52

Jenkinson, Anthony, 14; *map* of trade
    route, 13
Justices of the Peace, 41–2, 44

law and order, 42, 43–4
local government, 41
London, 17–22, 26; the plague, 37;
    beggars, 44; *map*, 53; London Bridge,
    19, 20

madrigal, 32
Mary Queen of Scots, 48–50
masque, 30
medicines, 36
militia, 44–5
music, 32

navy, 46–7, 51–2; conditions at sea, 15–16
Netherlands, 45, 46, 51
Nombre de Dios, 7, 57
North-East and North-West Passages, 11
New World (America), 7, 8, 9; colonies
    in, 14

Our Lady of the Conception, 10

Pacific Ocean, 10, 12
Panama, 7, 11
Parliament, 39
perfumes, 29
Persia, trade with, 14; *map*, 13
Philip II of Spain, 50
plague, 20, 36
Plymouth, 11, 51; *map*, 13, 53
potatoes, 14
progresses, 39
punishments, 42, 43–4
Puritans, 41

Raleigh, Sir Walter, 14; *illus.* 59
recipes, 31

recreations, 32–3
religion, *see* Church; Roman Catholics
Revenge, 52
roads, 23
Roman Catholics, 40, 48–50, 55
Royal Exchange, 17, 18
ruff, 27–8
Russia, trade with, 14; *map*, 13

St. Paul's Church, 18
St. Peter's Abbey, 17, 18
schools, 34–5
Scotland, 48, 52, 57
sea power, 58
Shakespeare, William, 21
sheep-farming, 23–4, 43
ships, 15, 46, 52; *illus.* 10
Sidney, Sir Philip, 45
slave trade, 9, 59
sorcerers, 35
Spain, 48; raids against, 7–10; war against,
    45, 50–3; *map*, 13
sports, 33, 22
Strait of Magellan, 10; *map*, 13
superstitions, 35–6

tableware, 29
Thames, River, 17, 19
theatres, 21
Tilbury, 56; *illus.* 55; *map*, 53
tobacco, 14; *illus.* 59
tooth-pullers, 36
towns, *see* London; 22
trade routes and trading companies, 14;
    trade with Spain, 9
trades, 20; *see also* industries

Ulster, 54; *map*, 53
unemployment, 43
universities, 34

villages, 23–4
Virginia, 14; *map*, 13

watch, the, 42
West Indies, 8; trade with, 9; *map*, 13
Whitehall, 38
wigs, 28
witchcraft, 35